· REDISCOVERING RAILWAYS ·

WEST SUSSEX

London Brighton & South Coast Rly.

LITTLEHAMPTON. (160)

From

To *Biddenham*

Via *Hastings*

Truck No. *2360*   Sheet No. *4*

Consignee *Pulbo*

Date *10 — 9 — 06*

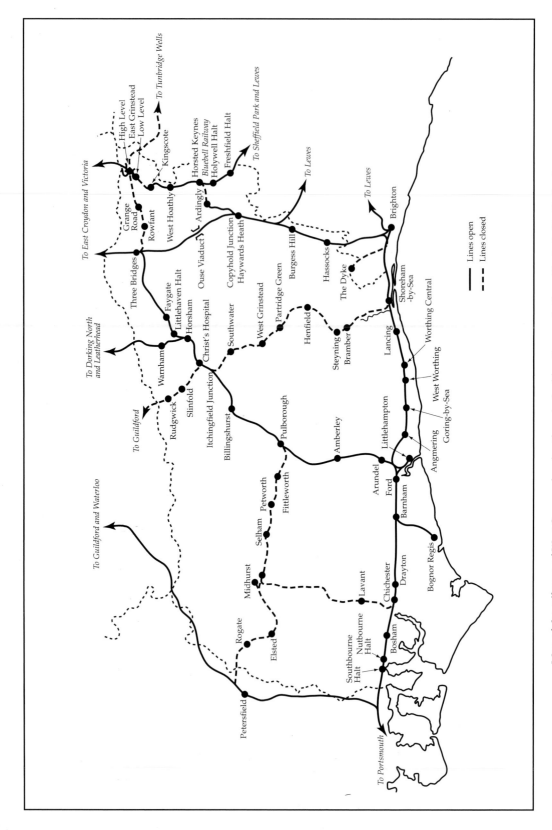

Map of the railways of West Sussex, showing the principal locations and others illustrated in the book.

• REDISCOVERING RAILWAYS •

WEST SUSSEX

A pictorial record of the county's railways past and present

Terry Gough

London Brighton & South Coast Railway.

Fay Gate to

ex Roffey Road Halt, Fay Gate.

• RAILWAY HERITAGE •
from
The NOSTALGIA *Collection*

First published in 2002

British Library Cataloguing in Publication Data

A catalogue record for this book is available from the British Library.

ISBN 1 85895 212 3

Past & Present Publishing Ltd
The Trundle
Ringstead Road
Great Addington
Kettering
Northants NN14 4BW

Tel/Fax: 01536 330588
email: sales@nostalgiacollection.com
Website: www.nostalgiacollection.com

Some of the material in this book first appeared in *British Railways Past and Present, No 18 Surrey and West Sussex*, by the same author and published by Past & Present Publishing Ltd in 1993.

All tickets and other items of ephemera are from the author's collection, and all photographs are by the author unless otherwise credited.

Printed and bound in Great Britain

Past and Present

A Past & Present book
from
The NOSTALGIA Collection

CONTENTS

WEST GRINSTEAD: The approach to the station from Horsham was, and indeed still is, attractive, except that today walking or cycling is the mode of transport, rather than the train. On 27 July 1963 Class 2MT No 41312 enters the station on the 1.21pm from Horsham.

There is still plenty of evidence of a railway, although for many years this view was completely obliterated by vegetation; however, all this was cleared to make way for the Downs Link bridleway.

EAST GRINSTEAD HIGH LEVEL: Set 758, consisting of ex-LBSCR coaches, is propelled into East Grinstead High Level station by Class M7 No 30109 on 2 May 1958. The train is the 10.49am from Three Bridges, which will terminate here.

The High Level station site is almost unrecognisable now, although beyond the far end of the car park the trackbed has been used for a bridleway and cyclepath known as the Worth Way.

INTRODUCTION

This book arose from a previous book in the 'British Railways Past and Present' series in which I covered Surrey and West Sussex. There are so many railway lines within these two counties that the opportunity has been taken to devote a complete book to West Sussex alone.

Railways came very early to the county and many are still open. There have, as everywhere in the country, been closures, but much of the system built in Victorian times has survived. The more important lines were electrified before the Second World War, and the ever-increasing population along the South Coast has resulted in sufficient passenger traffic to require frequent services both along the coast and to London, and new halts have been added along the coast to meet the needs of people moving to the expanding towns. Inland the population spread is variable, with concentrations along the Brighton to London line and in the Horsham area. The Mid-Sussex line, on the other hand, passes through less populated areas and serves smaller towns, while the branch lines radiating from Horsham (to both Guildford and Brighton) and from Midhurst have been closed. The short branch to The Dyke has also gone. Nonetheless, overall the county has faired very well and a sound future for the railways seems certain.

In preparing this revised volume I revisited most of the locations previously covered. Where there has been no significant change I have retained the original 'past' and 'present' pairs of photographs, while in the few cases where change has taken place, I have either added a third matching photograph or made an appropriate comment. I have endeavoured to cover almost all the stations in the county and there are therefore a number of locations included for the first time.

It has been an enjoyable experience revisiting places first seen about 40 years ago. In those days I travelled by bicycle and train, and the train was also used for the present-day visits wherever possible. Although the closed stations were reached by car, I still travelled by train from my home in Dorset to the nearest railhead, from where I hired a car.

Terry Gough
Sherborne, Dorset

ACKNOWLEDGEMENTS

Acknowledgements are due most importantly to my wife Cynthia who accompanied me on some of the 'past' occasions, not realising at the time that she was engaged on what would be an historic series of visits. On the recent trips she has given valuable input as a map-reader and adviser in aligning the 'past' and 'present' perspectives. I am grateful for help given by Colin Pattle and Dick Ware, to the various owners of former railway stations, and to the railway authorities for the provision of a lineside pass. There were a few 'past' locations for which I had no material, and for photographs of these I thank James Aston, the late John Smith (Lens of Sutton) and John Stretton. Lawrence Golden, as ever, willingly supplied colour photographs for the cover.

BIBLIOGRAPHY

The Bluebell Railway, Terry Gough (Past & Present Publishing, 1998)

Forgotten Railways: South East England, H. P. White (David & Charles, 1976)

Rediscovering Railways: Surrey, The east of the county, Terry Gough (Past & Present Publishing, in preparation)

Rediscovering Railways: Surrey, The west of the county, Terry Gough (Past & Present Publishing, 2002)

Southern Railway Reflections: Branch Lines Recalled, Terry Gough (Silver Link Publishing, 1999)

Southern Railway Reflections: Kent and Sussex, Terry Gough (Silver Link Publishing, in preparation)

Southern Railway Reflections: Surrey and Berkshire, Terry Gough (Silver Link Publishing, 1999)

A Southern Region Chronology & Record, R. H. Clarke (Oakwood Press, 1964 and 1975)

Three Bridges to Tunbridge Wells, David Gould (Oakwood Press, 1983)

To The Railway Born, Tony Carter (Silver Link Publishing, 1992; deals in part with the Steyning line)

GUILDFORD AND BRIGHTON LINES FROM HORSHAM

CHRIST'S HOSPITAL (1) was where the branch from Guildford met the Mid-Sussex line from Horsham to Arundel, seen in the background. Three platforms were provided exclusively for the Guildford trains, rather excessive bearing in mind the infrequent service. The Mid-Sussex line platforms (numbers 1, 2 and 3) are out of sight to the right, as Class H No 31308 moves away with a morning train from Guildford on 24 March 1968.

In 1992 there was still clear evidence of the branch platforms, and the signal box is still in use. Even the semaphore signal has survived.

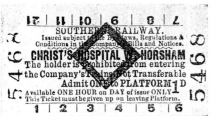

CHRIST'S HOSPITAL (2): The locomotive is again No 31308, on the return working to Guildford, which left Horsham at 9.30am. The station is immediately on the far side of the bridge.

The more recent view shows that the bridge, which carries a farm track, is still in place. The footpath alongside the old trackbed leads to the Downs Link, a bridleway that links the North and South Downs Ways and uses 30 miles of disused railway line.

SLINFOLD had a small station, with not even a passing loop. On 27 July 1963 the 10.34am Guildford to Horsham train consists of Class 2MT No 41223 and BR Mark I coaches. Although the village of Slinfold was nearby, the station saw very little traffic, particularly in later years.

The site is now far busier, at least during the summer, as it is a caravan site. There is no trace of the station building, but the attractive rows of trees that were to the left of the train and behind the station have been retained.

RUDGWICK was the next station up the line, and we get a clear view of the railway from the embankment at the Horsham end in March 1961. In the first view Class 2MT No 41303 works the 9.22am from Guildford, consisting of an SR 10-compartment all-3rd coach and two Maunsell ex-main-line coaches.

By July 1963, the date of the second photograph, the railway was beginning to look derelict, despite still being open. The line survived for another two years, and by 1968 really was derelict, as seen in the third picture.

Development of the site came a few years later, when the station building was replaced by a general practitioners' surgery. The station approach road is now lined with houses and the yard throat is occupied by a block of flats, just visible on the right. Throughout all these changes the Victorian house in the background has stood firm.

CHRIST'S HOSPITAL (3): We now return to Christ's Hospital, where the junction for Brighton was to the south of the station and the Horsham to Brighton trains shared the main platforms with the Arundel and Bognor Regis services. In March 1960 the 9.30am Brighton to Horsham train consists of Class M7 No 30049 and push-pull set No 714. The signal box seen in the photographs on page 9 is visible in the background.

The track layout and station buildings have been much simplified and EMU No 1859 of Class 421/4 stands in exactly the same place as the push-pull train above. All the main station buildings have been demolished and the far face of the island platform is now the down platform. The railings for the subway connecting the former island platform are just visible in the right centre of the photograph.

SOUTHWATER: This is the view looking towards Brighton on 24 July 1960, as Class H No 31543 enters the station on the 10.30am to Horsham.

In the spring of 1992 all that was left of the station was the crumbling edge of the down platform, the drain in the foreground and a footpath where the boarded crossing was once located. The cottages on the extreme left are still standing, but hidden from view by bushes. The goods yard has given way to a small factory.

WEST GRINSTEAD: Heading for Brighton on 23 March 1960 is the 1.19pm from Horsham propelled by Class M7 No 30052. The main station building is at a higher level to the right and still stood in 1992, as did the attractive trees on the opposite side of the line.

PARTRIDGE GREEN (1): Class Q heavy freight locomotives were rarely seen on passenger trains other than specials, and the appearance of No 30545 at Partridge Green, hauling a Brighton to Bristol excursion on 30 July 1960, was unexpected.

The station site is now a housing estate and almost the only evidence that there was once a railway here is the foundations of the goods shed on the left. The garden fence parallels the site of the up platform.

PARTRIDGE GREEN (2): The 2.21pm train from Horsham to Brighton enters Partridge Green behind Class 2MT No 41230 on 27 July 1963. The use of main-line corridor coaches on secondary routes and branches was quite common in the 1960s, as pre-Grouping wooden-bodied coaches were withdrawn.

    The location of the station was deduced from the nearby road, as virtually nothing remains of the railway itself.

HENFIELD: This view is very similar to the 'past' photograph opposite, but it is a different station. This is Henfield, and the 10.21am train from Horsham to Brighton on 7 September 1965 is hauled by Class 2MT No 41299.

This is another location where the railway has been completely obliterated, as seen in 1999. The road that used to pass over the railway is behind the house across the end of the cul-de-sac. *J. H. Aston/TG*

STEYNING (1) was one of the more important stations on the line and engines took water here. Class M7 No 30049 is on the 11.37am Brighton to Horsham service in July 1960.

The trackbed is now the Steyning bypass, on which a 1930s car looks rather out of place in 1992. The site is easily recognised by the handsome three-storey building on the right, which has been converted into offices. A small museum in the town contains a number of local railway exhibits.

REDISCOVERING RAILWAYS

STEYNING (2): Another M7, No 30052, at the other end of Steyning station, takes water in preparation for completing its journey to Brighton in 1960. Note how, in order to do this, the train had to be propelled beyond the platform end.

In the present-day photograph the main identifying features are the house on the left and the two bridges, although the one in the foreground has been completely renewed.

BRAMBER was only half a mile from Steyning. A down train propelled by Class H No 31322 waits to proceed to Brighton in the summer of 1960.

All evidence of the station has been obliterated by a roundabout and new road construction. These major changes make it difficult to judge exactly the location of the station, but its approximate position was in the hollow between the fence and the road embankment.

DORKING NORTH AND THREE BRIDGES LINES FROM HORSHAM

HORSHAM (1), the next station north from Christ's Hospital, is a major station on the Mid-Sussex line, but the most interesting trains were the steam-operated services to Guildford and Brighton. On 24 March 1961 Class E4 No 32475 waits to leave on the 6.00pm to Brighton.

The 1992 scene is clearly of the same location, but the steam stock has given way to EMUs Nos 6334 and others of Class 416, which were designed by the SR; however, since this photograph was taken these units have also passed into history. Demolition of the building on the right is in progress.

Left HORSHAM (2): Steam and electric trains were regularly seen together at Horsham. Class M7 No 30047 has just arrived with the 10.08am push-pull train from Brighton, while to the left is 4SUB electric unit No 4734 on a London-bound train. The stock on the right is part of a special train from London to Midhurst on 8 June 1958.

Horsham station has changed very little, but the trains are different. Fast trains from London via Three Bridges are usually formed of BR-built corridor slam-door stock such as this unit, No 1716 of Class 4CIG (421). Trains from London via Leatherhead and Dorking North are usually modern suburban stock such as Class 455.

London Brighton & South Coast Railway.

Waldron and Horeham Road to

Horsham

HORSHAM SHED was a half-roundhouse with an allocation of engines for the passenger services to Brighton and Guildford, and for local freight workings. On 9 October 1955 the shed houses Classes E4 No 32470, Q No 30534, M7 No 30048 and C2X No 32523. The shed closed to steam in 1959 and completely in 1964.

A visit in the summer of 1999 found the site occupied by offices and a car park. The exact location was deduced from surrounding railway huts and remnants of trackwork.

WARNHAM: This 1960s view of Warnham shows the traditional signal box and gates still in operation, and a visit in May 1992 found that nothing substantial had changed as Class 2EPB (416) No 6324 worked a Dorking to Horsham train.

LITTLEHAVEN HALT is only a mile from Horsham towards Three Bridges, and was built by the LBSCR in 1907 for motor-train services. The station is seen here in 1968.

Almost nothing of the original station remains. Wood and corrugated iron have given way to concrete and glass, although the level crossing gates have yet to be replaced by automatic barriers. Class 423 No 3501 leaves the station dead on time on a Horsham to Victoria train on 11 April 1992.

FAYGATE: This early photograph depicts a typical small LBSCR country station. Although today the main buildings have gone, the signal box remains, boarded up and daubed with spray paint. Faygate is only served by trains during the rush-hour periods, unlike Littlehaven and Ifield, which have a regular service throughout the day. *Lens of Sutton/TG*

REDISCOVERING RAILWAYS

MID-SUSSEX LINE

BILLINGSHURST is seen here looking south well before the days of electrification. The present-day (July 1999) view shows remarkably little major change. The station buildings and footbridge are still in use, as is the signal box at the country end of the station. Billingshurst has an hourly service between Victoria and Bognor Regis/Portsmouth Harbour, with additional trains during the rush hour. *Lens of Sutton/TG*

PULBOROUGH was the junction for the Midhurst line. This view of the main line looking north was taken in SR days after electrification. This is another station where the main buildings, including the signal box, have survived in railway use. On 28 July 1999 Class 4CIG (421) No 1837 enters the station forming the 09.18 service from Victoria to Littlehampton. *Lens of Sutton/TG*

AMBERLEY is the next station southwards on the Mid-Sussex line, which was electrified in 1938, so steam passenger workings were rarely seen thereafter. On 18 October 1964 Class Q No 30530 works a railway enthusiasts' special past Amberley en route to Littlehampton.

Apart from the loss of the goods shed and part of the main building, Amberley has not changed much in over 30 years. However, nothing more interesting than EMU No 1718 of Class 421 forms a Victoria to Bognor Regis and Portsmouth Harbour service on 4 April 1992. Prior to 1978 trains from London were routed via Sutton, but since then have taken the Brighton main line as far as Three Bridges in order to serve Gatwick Airport.

NEAR ARUNDEL: The countryside becomes flat, but still attractive, as the railway nears Arundel. The unit on the rear of this Bognor Regis to Horsham train on 24 May 1958 is 2BIL No 2146.

Little of substance has changed to detract from the view in 1992 other than the rolling-stock, which is Class 421 No 1850 forming the 12.36 Portsmouth Harbour to Victoria service on 4 April.

REDISCOVERING RAILWAYS

ARUNDEL: An up train in pre-Grouping days is hauled by a Class B2X 4-4-0 passenger engine, built originally as Class B2 just before the turn of the century. The scene is instantly recognisable in 1999, with a 1960s-design train consisting of Class 4CIG (421) No 1727. Despite the time indicated by the station clock, it was 08.15 and the train was the 07.59 from Bognor Regis to Victoria. The canopy on the down side was added by the SR. *Lens of Sutton/TG*

MIDHURST BRANCHES

FITTLEWORTH: Class Q No 30530 stops at Fittleworth on a special train from London on 18 October 1964 en route to Midhurst. The station is in the right background beyond the small wooden goods shed.

  The station and grounds are now in private ownership and the goods shed and main buildings still exist, the latter beautifully maintained.

PETWORTH station is seen on 22 July 1961, six years after the withdrawal of passenger services. Freight services continued sporadically for several years.

The main station building has since been restored and is used for a bed and breakfast business. Edmondson-style 'tickets' advertising the facilities are available, as illustrated below. In October 1998 two 1st Class Pullman coaches were delivered to the station yard and these provide superior accommodation. The coaches, *Alicante* and *Mimosa*, came from Marazion and before then had been used on the Southern Region.

Ticket for the 'West Sussex Downsman', 8 June 1958

SELHAM (1) was the last station travelling west towards Midhurst, and an excellent view was obtained from a nearby hill. In late 1964 I watched an excursion train hauled by a Class Q approach from Midhurst.

By the spring of 1992 the view had become completely obstructed, but the location can be identified by the bridge abutment, being that in the right foreground of the 'past' picture. The station still stands, but is no longer visible from this location.

SELHAM (2): Another excursion is seen this time at the other end of the station. The train is hauled by two ex-LBSCR engines, Class E4 No 32503 and E6 No 32417, and is heading toward Midhurst on 24 June 1962.

In contrast to the east of the station seen opposite, this location is still readily recognisable and the station is clearly visible in the background.

MIDHURST (1) was the junction for three branch lines. To the east trains ran to Pulborough, to the west they terminated at Petersfield, while the line running south joined the coast route near Chichester. The LSWR and LBSCR each had a station at Midhurst, but the SR closed the former in 1925. The Pulborough and Petersfield services were both withdrawn on 7 February 1955, but Pulborough to Midhurst was retained for several more years, during which time occasional specials were run, as we have already seen. Here Class Q No 30530 arrives at Midhurst in the autumn of 1964 with a railway enthusiasts' special, to the amazement of the local people.

The site of Midhurst station is difficult to locate as the area has been transformed by housing development. The present-day view is from the same location as far as can be estimated, the line of houses following approximately the trackbed.

MIDHURST (2): Seen from the opposite direction, looking west from above the tunnel mouth, is the empty carriage stock from a ramblers' excursion leaving Midhurst for Horsham behind Class Q No 30549 on 8 June 1958. The tunnel mouth still exists and served once again as a vantage point for the present-day photograph.

ELSTED station was the first beyond Midhurst in the Petersfield direction, and looked forlorn in 1958, just three years after closure. The building stood for many more years until making way for industrial development. Although both views were taken from the adjacent road bridge, there is little to link them, except the roof of the cottages in the background.

REDISCOVERING RAILWAYS

ROGATE was the only other intermediate station on the Midhurst-Petersfield line. The original main station building still stands and is used as the offices for a firm of architects. At the time of my visit (July 1999) an extension was being constructed on the Midhurst end of the building. *Lens of Sutton/TG*

LAVANT (1) was the last station before Chichester on the line from Midhurst. Passenger services were withdrawn in 1935, but the line from Chichester to Lavant was retained for seasonal freight and occasional special passenger trains. One of the latter, yet again worked by Class Q locomotives, on this occasion Nos 30531 and 30543, is seen just south of Lavant and heading toward Chichester on the evening of 3 November 1963.

The field to the left later became a quarry for road stone. The line was diverted to serve the quarry and re-opened in 1972, carrying four trains per day until closure on 15 March 1991. On 27 July 1990 the stone train is worked by Class 73 electro-diesel No 73141. The course of the original line is identified by the overbridge above the locomotive; in the 'past' photograph this is immediately behind the train.

The quarry has since closed and the railway dismantled. The third view is dated July 1999, and shows that the cutting has been filled in. The trackbed is now the Centurion Way, a cyclepath to Chichester. The bridge still exists and is guarded by 'centurions', made ingeniously from gas cylinders, chairs and other ironmongery.

REDISCOVERING RAILWAYS

LAVANT (2): On 23 May 1958 there was still evidence of activity at Lavant station, with a few wagons in the yard. The freight service ceased on 5 August 1968 and the station was left unoccupied for many years. In 1992 renovation began and the station subsequently formed part of a housing association development called 'The Hunting Gate'.

BRIGHTON MAIN LINE

THREE BRIDGES (1) station was built by the SR and is a similar age to 2BIL electric unit No 2149, seen on 9 October 1955 long before the days of yellow cab ends.

Little has changed in this 10 April 1992 view, which features Class 421 No 1837 leaving the station forming the 15.00 Brighton to Victoria stopping train.

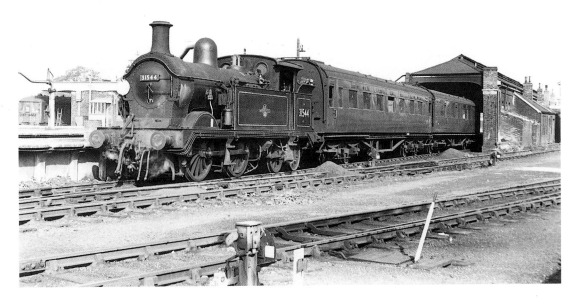

THREE BRIDGES (2): The other side of the station was much more interesting, where the East Grinstead trains used the far platform with its overall roof, a remnant of the old station. On 7 October 1962 Class H No 31544 waits to leave with the 11.08am push-pull train.

This is the only part of Three Bridges station to have changed significantly. The old buildings have been swept away and the branch taken up, and the area is now most unwelcoming.

THREE BRIDGES JUNCTION: Three Bridges was also the junction for Horsham and the Mid-Sussex line. On 22 April 1961 Class K No 32342 shunts a few wagons on the Horsham line.

The view was no more attractive on 11 April 1992 as Class 09 shunter No 09006 runs light en route to the Horsham line.

THREE BRIDGES SHED was situated in the vee of the junction, and had an allocation of predominantly ex-LBSCR engines to work the Central Division's freight trains; the only passenger engines allocated there were for the East Grinstead branch. Visible on shed on 9 October 1955 are two Class K 2-6-0s, Nos 32353 and 32345, while behind the former are two Class C2X 0-6-0s. Adjacent to the shed was an extensive engineers' yard, and this is still in use.

The track layout has been changed, but this is the view taken in May 1986 from the same position as the 'past' photograph. In the distance, just to the right of the corrugated maintenance shed, is the sub-station shown on the previous page, but looking from the opposite direction.

OUSE VALLEY VIADUCT: SR Class CC electric locomotive No 20003 on a Victoria to Newhaven boat train on 17 September 1966 crosses the Ouse Valley Viaduct, between Balcombe and Haywards Heath.

The viaduct still makes an imposing sight, even though the trains are less interesting. On 11 April 1992 a dual-voltage EMU of Class 319 passes over the viaduct as the 08.40 Bedford to Brighton service.

COPYHOLD JUNCTION (1) was a short distance south of the viaduct, and passing on 15 September 1963 is the down 'Brighton Belle' formed by Pullman electric unit No 3052. The line on the right then offered an alternative between Brighton and London, although it was only electrified as far as Horsted Keynes.

A train of somewhat inferior stock, the 10.32 Victoria to Brighton semi-fast, passes the site of the junction in April 1992.

COPYHOLD JUNCTION (2): On 15 September 1963 2HAL No 2674 leaves the branch with a service from Horsted Keynes to Seaford.

Passenger services on the branch were withdrawn in October 1963 and it was cut back to Ardingly. It is still used for stone trains, but the junction has been taken out and trains run on their own line as far as Haywards Heath, before reversing and running back through Copyhold on the main line. On 16 July 1992 Class 59 No 59101 approaches en route to Southall.

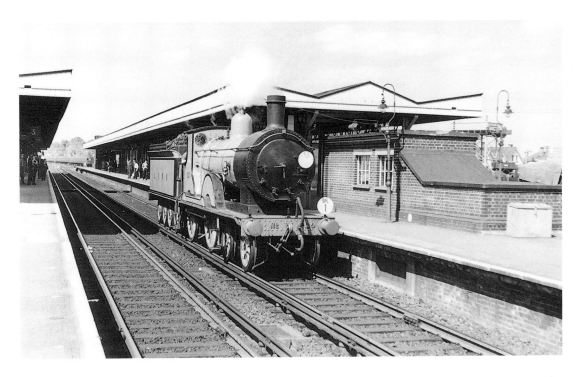

HAYWARDS HEATH: A glimpse of steam in the heart of the SR electrified system is provided on 24 June 1962 by preserved Class T9 No 120 in LSWR livery, passing through the station on its way to work a special train. Haywards Heath station was rebuilt by the SR in 1932.

There are only two non-electric passenger trains per day, both operated by Virgin Trains. On 22 March 2002 the 07.15 Manchester Piccadilly to Brighton train arrived 5 minutes early and was put in the far platform to avoid blocking the main line. The stock consists of Class 220 Nos 220013 and 220006. Thameslink Class 319 No 319214 passes the Virgin train on the late-running 10.42 Bedford to Brighton service.

BURGESS HILL: The 1.02pm parcels train from London Bridge to Brighton passes through the station, worked by electro-diesel Class 73 No E6025 (later 73119) on 19 September 1966.

On 28 July 1999 Class 4CIG (421) No 1709 stops at Burgess Hill forming the 14.32 Victoria to Brighton semi-fast train. *J. H. Aston/TG*

HASSOCKS: We are looking south in the early days of electrification. The sidings beyond the signal box were used to store condemned SR electric units displaced by BR-built EMUs in the late 1950s.

Up and down trains cross on 22 March 2002. The Thameslink train on the left is the 12.12 Bedford to Brighton, consisting of Class 319 No 319218. On the right the Virgin Trains 14.18 Brighton to Manchester Piccadilly service is formed of Class 220 Nos 220006 and 220013. *Lens of Sutton/TG*

THREE BRIDGES TO EAST GRINSTEAD

Opposite THREE BRIDGES: An excellent view of departing trains, with the signal box in the background, was provided a few hundred yards on to the East Grinstead branch. This part of the line now forms a road, but the location is recognisable by the pylons in the background.

ROWFANT: The Three Bridges to East Grinstead High Level line ran through a sparsely populated area, with two intermediate stations. This is Rowfant, where on 9 September 1961 the push-pull train to Three Bridges hauled by Class H No 31551 passes light engine No 32348 of Class K.

The line closed in 1967, and by 1986 the track, crossing gates and signal box had all been removed. Despite this the location was still easily recognisable.

A visit in the summer of 1999 found the buildings in use, but the trackbed could no longer be seen from the road. The land immediately to the south of the station is occupied by a gas supply company.

GRANGE ROAD: Push-pull set No 602, forming the 4.27pm from East Grinstead, pauses at Grange Road on 3 June 1960. The line has since been given over to allotments; it ran between the gap in the buildings in the left background beyond the large tree. The buildings themselves are relatively new and all trace of the station has gone.

EAST GRINSTEAD HIGH LEVEL (1): Class 4MT No 42091 rounds the steeply graded approach to the High Level station with the 10.08am from Victoria on 16 March 1958. The sharpness of the curve necessitated the location of the outer home on the up side of the line.

The High Level station closed on 2 January 1967. The view is now totally obscured by trees, and the area is a car park whose perimeter is marked out using old rails – the ultimate insult!

EAST GRINSTEAD HIGH LEVEL (2): This is the west end on 3 June 1960, looking east. On the far left is a train from London, while the 5.47pm Tunbridge Wells West to Victoria waits to leave behind Class 4MT No 80017. On the extreme right is the push-pull train to Three Bridges.

The High Level site is almost unrecognisable in 1999. Beyond the extreme end of the car park the railway embankment has been removed to make way for a new road (see opposite).

EAST GRINSTEAD HIGH LEVEL (3): Class 4MT No 42067 approaches the east end of High Level Station on the 10.47am from Tunbridge Wells West on 2 May 1958.

Here is another total transformation, with almost all of the railway having been removed. There are no landmarks linking these two views, and the only clues are behind the photographer, rather than in the viewfinder.

EAST GRINSTEAD AND THE BLUEBELL RAILWAY

EAST GRINSTEAD LOW LEVEL (1): Class 2MT No 41319 at the head of a London-bound train waits to leave East Grinstead Low Level in the final years of the BR service from Brighton.

The location now looks very different as the footbridge and bridge carrying the High Level line have both been removed. On 17 February 1996 Class 4VEP (423) No 3514 leaves for Victoria. *Lens of Sutton/TG*

EAST GRINSTEAD LOW LEVEL (2): BR Standard Class 4MT No 80154 is seen at the south end of the station on the last day of operations to Lewes. Even in 1958 there was an air of desolation, although the carriage sidings and goods yard were still in use.

The identical view in 1992 shows that the yards have gone and the town of East Grinstead has acquired a completely different skyline. Two London trains can be seen in the station. The single line in the foreground, which terminates just behind the camera, is used for storing stock outside the peak periods. It is this point that the Bluebell Railway will eventually reach, thus re-uniting Horsted Keynes (page 65) with the main network.

KINGSCOTE: In September 1961, six years after the closure of Kingscote station, everything is still in place as if waiting for the service to be re-instated.

In the May 1986 photograph the station is still waiting and in the intervening years the downside buildings have been demolished. However, the Bluebell Railway later repaired the remaining buildings and installed platform lighting in readiness for the restoration of services, which took place in April 1994. A visit in appalling weather in the winter of 1996 found that a transformation into an active station had taken place.

Opposite WEST HOATHLY (closed in 1958) also stood abandoned for many years, as can be seen in the 'past' photograph taken in July 1962.

Unfortunately the site was subsequently cleared, leaving only the platform edges and of course the tunnel to identify the location. By early 1992, however, the Bluebell Railway had relaid the track to West Hoathly, although no station facilities have been provided. On 26 June 1992 preserved SR Class U No 1618 passes with a train from Sheffield Park.

REDISCOVERING RAILWAYS

HORSTED KEYNES (1) was the junction for the electrified line to Copyhold Junction and Haywards Heath on the Brighton main line. Looking north, a pair of 2NOLs, Nos 1844 and 1821, have just arrived forming the 10.25am from Seaford on 11 May 1958.

The 1992 view shows that electric trains have been superseded by steam! My camera bag (on the platform on the right of the 'past' view) has long since expired, and in the present climate would not be left lying around on platforms. No 1618 is seen again on a Bluebell Railway train.

HORSTED KEYNES (2): In the early days of the re-opening as the Bluebell Railway, Class A1X No 32655 (*Stepney*), repainted in LBSCR livery, enters Horsted Keynes from the south with ex-Chesham Line wooden-bodied coaches on a train from Sheffield Park.

Thirty years later, on 11 April 1992, the train from Sheffield Park is worked by Class H No 263. The foreground is almost unchanged, but to the left of the platforms the derelict yard is now occupied by a carriage shed.

HORSTED KEYNES (3): Prior to obtaining running powers into what was then Horsted Keynes BR station, the Bluebell Railway terminated at a temporary station a few yards to the south, and trains were run between there and Sheffield Park with an engine at each end. On 15 July 1961 the train was worked by Class P Nos 323 *Bluebell* and 27. The coach on the extreme right by the road bridge served as offices for the railway.

A much tidier scene is evident in April 1992, the only remaining identifying feature being the road bridge. There is no sign that there was ever a station here.

HOLYWELL HALT: Similar changes have taken place here, where in 1962 there was a halt. Class A1X No 55 *Stepney* and Class P No 27 are seen near the station on 31 July.

In the summer of 1992 there is no evidence of the halt, the motive power is somewhat more powerful and the rolling-stock is steel-bodied main-line stock.

FRESHFIELD HALT: On 15 July 1961 a Sheffield Park train, hauled by Class P No 323 and pushed by Class 0415 No 488, stops at the platform.

The halt closed in 1989 and no trace remains. In April 1992 Class H No 263 passes the location on a mixed train consisting of Maunsell SR and LSWR coaches and a few wagons.

ARDINGLY (1) was the only intermediate station between Horsted Keynes and Haywards Heath, and is seen here looking towards Haywards Heath on 3 March 1934, a year prior to electrification.

The site is now occupied by a stone depot, which has obliterated the platforms. At first sight it seems as though there is no rail connection, but the track has been slewed a few yards to the right and runs behind the staithes, as seen in the third photograph. Taken on 13 March 1996, it shows Class 59 No 59103 arriving with empty wagons from Acton. *H. C. Casserley/TG (2)*

2nd Special Day Excursion 2nd
(C.M. 16735) 11th MAY 1958
THE BLUEBELL SPECIAL
Clapham Junction to
HORSTED KEYNES & ARDINGLY
Via Dormans
AND BACK
(8) For conditions over

ARDINGLY (2): On 21 October 1962 EMU Class 2HAL No 2657 stops in the hope of passengers. The station was closed to passengers in October the following year and the line toward Horsted Keynes dismantled.

SOUTH COAST LINE

SOUTHBOURNE HALT was typical of many halts along the South Coast. Some were built by the LBSCR and others were added or rebuilt by the SR as the population along the coast increased and bungalow towns were built. The

nearer corrugated iron hut is the booking office; most of the halts had a booking office on both the up and down platforms, each having a separately identifiable platform ticket issue.

Southbourne is still a busy station and on 19 June 1992 several passengers have just disembarked from the 11.36 Portsmouth Harbour to Victoria train, provided by EMU Class 421 No 1711.

NUTBOURNE HALT was very similar and the basic facilities are seen from a passing train in 1970.

By 1992 minor improvements had been made, but there is still the feeling of desolation, particularly in winter, despite the proximity of factories and houses. On 19 June 1992 Class 73 Nos 73126 *Kent & East Sussex Railway* and 73133 *The Bluebell Railway* double-head a ballast train towards Chichester.

BOSHAM was a more substantial station, with a level crossing at the west end. Most surprisingly, the semaphore signals and level crossing gates still survived in June 1992, although they were replaced later in the year as part of a modernisation programme between Chichester and Havant. Class 421 No 1749 approaches Bosham forming the 10.14 Portsmouth Harbour to Brighton train on 19 June.

The new level crossing barriers and signal are shown in this July 1999 view. Note also the change to the footbridge steps on the right. The EMU is Class 4VEP (423) No 3811 forming a Basingstoke to Brighton service.

CHICHESTER YARD (1) in May 1988 finds Class 33 No 33028 shunting a few wagons. Much of the track had already been removed and it was not long before the yard closed. The land was subsequently sold and is now occupied by a supermarket. In the foreground is the main coast line.

The second photograph, taken on 19 June 1992, shows the supermarket under construction. In the foreground EMU Class 4VEP (423) No 1729 forms a train from Victoria to Portsmouth Harbour.

CHICHESTER YARD (2) is seen earlier in 1969 with recently withdrawn 6COR express electric unit No 3046 awaiting disposal. These SR units had all been displaced by new BR-designed CIG rolling-stock, now referred to as Class 421. The uninspiring present-day view shows the delivery reception area of the supermarket.

CHICHESTER: The undated 'past' photograph (probably early 1930s) shows a Midhurst train in the bay platform at Chichester. The station has since been rebuilt, but the site of the bay is easy to identify, as shown in the second view taken in the summer of 1999. *Lens of Sutton/TG*

DRAYTON: This is Drayton in LBSCR days with a double-headed train bound for Brighton. Drayton closed as early as 1930 and all remains of the station have now gone. The same place in July 1999 sees a very different train, in the shape of Class 158 No 158832 forming the 12.00 Cardiff Central to Brighton service. *Lens of Sutton/TG*

London Brighton and South Coast Railway.

Hartfield to

Drayton

BARNHAM: This general view of Barnham Junction station is looking toward Brighton in early SR days prior to electrification. The Bognor Regis line diverges immediately behind the camera.

The location is still recognisable today and on 28 July 1999 the 11.02 from Victoria is being divided at Barnham; the front half will leave at 12.39 for Portsmouth Harbour and the rear portion 2 minutes later for Bognor Regis. The trains consist of 4CIGs (421) Nos 1744 and 1734 respectively. *Lens of Sutton/TG*

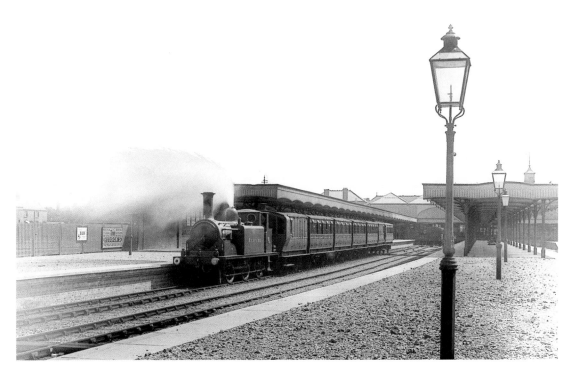

BOGNOR REGIS: This pre-Grouping view shows Class D1 No 228 *Seaford* and its train dwarfed by the station. The situation was not dissimilar on a visit in the summer of 1999, when EMU Class 4CIG (421) No 1734 hid in the depths of the station. *Lens of Sutton/TG*

FORD is the junction for the Littlehampton branch and in 1968 SR-built 2BIL EMU No 2082 works the shuttle service. The bay has long since been removed, but the Littlehampton line still has a frequent service of trains from Portsmouth, Brighton and London, although not all trains along the South Coast line stop at Ford. The South Coast also sees trains from much further afield, and on 16 May 1992 Class 158 No 158868 works the 05.53 Haverfordwest to Brighton service.

LITTLEHAMPTON: The view from the end of the platform is overshadowed by the SR signal gantry. In the background is the electric depot built by the SR in 1938.

As Class 421/1 No 1123 left on an afternoon train to Brighton in April 1992, it was surprising to find that the signals were still in use and, indeed, that there had been no major changes in the view from the end of the platform, although the station buildings have all been replaced. Another visit in 1999 confirmed that there had still been no changes to the signals.

ANGMERING (1): This photograph taken in LBSCR days shows a Class B2 4-4-0 heading a Brighton train. It must have been taken prior to 1916 because by this time all the class had been rebuilt as Class B2X.

On the right the main station building and the goods shed (behind the ladders) still exist, although on the Chichester side the original waiting room has given way to a 'bus shelter'. An SR concrete footbridge, semaphore signals and crossing barriers complete the major changes. The train is the 10.14 Littlehampton to Seaford, formed of Class 3COP (421) No 1409 *Operation Perseus*, which is unusual in two respects: first, because it is one of only 11 three-coach units recently formed from Class 4CIG specifically for the Portsmouth-Brighton line, and second, it was at the time of writing the only slam-door EMU to be named. *Lens of Sutton/TG*

ANGMERING (2): This is the view from the west end of the station in 1967. The 1999 view lacks both semaphore signals and signal box, although they were only removed a few years previously. Class 4CIG (421) No 1726 approaches the station as the 08.45 Bournemouth to Victoria semi-fast train on 28 July.

GORING-BY-SEA station building was much smaller than that at Angmering, but it did have a footbridge even in pre-Grouping days, and it generally gives the impression of being more a country than a seaside station. The platform canopy is a more recent addition, but both the up and down sides have retained the original buildings. The level crossing is used only by local traffic, as a road overbridge has been built at the east end of the station. Another Bournemouth-Victoria train (Class 4CIG No 1720) approaches on 29 July 1999. *Lens of Sutton/TG*

WEST WORTHING: An unidentified Class D1 enters the bay at the west end of West Worthing station. The guard's uniform and signal arms indicate the SR period, but the absence of conductor rails makes it earlier than 1938.

Electrification was extended westward from Worthing Central in 1938, and an electric train depot was built at West Worthing. This is now closed, but can be seen to the right of the approaching train, Class 3COP (421) No 1411 forming the 10.12 Portsmouth Harbour to Brighton service. *Lens of Sutton/TG*

WORTHING CENTRAL: No 3034, SR express electric stock of Class 6PAN, forms the front portion of the 10.09am Littlehampton to Victoria train on 21 June 1955.

The present-day train, in the form of a Class 158 unit, is comfortable, but lacks the sumptuous seating and high-quality fittings of the best SR-built trains. No 158869 leaves Worthing Central on the last few miles of its journey from Cardiff Central to Brighton. *J. H. Aston/TG*

LANCING: There have been dramatic changes at Lancing, where the main SR carriage works was located, employing about 2,000 people and occupying over 60 acres of land. On 8 June 1962 Class E4 No 32468 shunts in the works yard. The coast line is beyond the wooden fence in the background.

   Today almost all trace of the works has been removed and much of the site is occupied by houses and small industrial premises. Because the area is completely flat it is very difficult to identify earlier views. However, confirmation that this 1992 photograph is at the same location is given by the houses in the background and by the yard lamps to the left. Class 421/4 No 1867 forms the 11.46 East Worthing to Brighton service on 16 May.

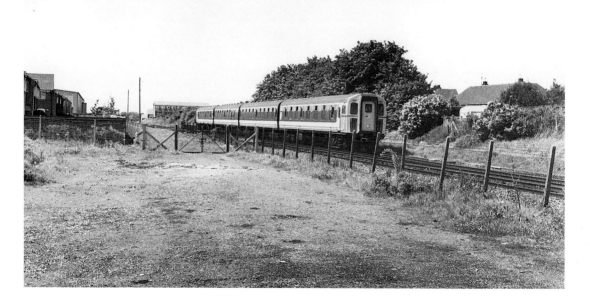

SHOREHAM BRIDGE on the River Adur is located just before the boundary between East and West Sussex. The junction for Horsham was just on the east side of the bridge and the branch ran for a short distance adjacent to the east bank of the river. On a winter afternoon in 1964 'Merchant Navy' Class No 35007 *Aberdeen Commonwealth* takes its train over the bridge to Brighton. There were regular steam-operated services on the coast line, usually worked by Bulleid 'Pacifics', at least in the summer months on through trains from the West Country.

Crossing the bridge on 4 April 1992 is a rather less interesting BR EMU. However, there are still through services on Sundays from as far away as Penzance.

THE DYKE branch left the coast line just west of Aldrington Halt, which together with much of the branch is in East Sussex; however, Devil's Dyke itself is in West Sussex. Unpublished photographs, particularly of the steam railcar that was built especially for the branch, are very rare, as it was only used for two years from 1933; it is seen here at the terminus at Easter 1934.

The second 'past' photograph (undated) shows a conventional train waiting to leave for Brighton. This must have been a special occasion because the train usually consisted of only one coach.

The station site is now occupied by a farm, but there are clear indications of a former railway line. The curved approach is easily identifiable and at the extreme end of the line there are still the remnants of a goods platform. This is the view looking towards Brighton from the old trackbed at the station. *Ken Weaver/John Stretton collection/TG*

GAZETTEER OF WEST SUSSEX'S RAILWAYS

Mileages are taken from the Southern Railway Standard Timetable, 30 September 1935, where possible.

Lines from Horsham

Horsham to Guildford (LBSCR to Peasmarsh Junction)

Stations: Christ's Hospital West Horsham (2¼m from Horsham), Slinfold (4¾m), Rudgwick (7m). Other stations in Surrey.

Opening and closure: Stammerham Junction (West Horsham) to Peasmarsh Junction opened 2.10.1865. There was no station at Stammerham Junction until 28.4.1902 when Christ's Hospital West Horsham was opened. Slinfold opened with the line, and Rudgwick the following month; both closed 14.6.1965 when the line also closed completely.

Route and traffic: Between Horsham and West Horsham there were trains for the three lines to Guildford, Brighton and the Mid-Sussex line (Arundel and Littlehampton). At West Horsham the Guildford line turned sharply west into its own platforms. The line ran north-west along fairly flat ground as far as Slinfold, after which it dropped before reaching Rudgwick. Passenger trains were usually push-pull operated with ex-LBSCR tank engines and latterly BR-built engines, some of which were also push-pull fitted. Trains were approximately every other hour, with extra trains on the Surrey section of the line from Cranleigh. There was a daily freight service operated by engines of both LSWR and LBSCR origin. The line also saw occasional special passenger trains, but overall the traffic was light and few passengers used the two intermediate stations on a regular basis.

Horsham to Brighton (LBSCR)

Stations: Christ's Hospital (2¼m from Horsham), Itchingfield Junction (no station; 3m), Southwater (4½m), West Grinstead (7¾m), Partridge Green (9¾m), Henfield (11¾m), Steyning (15½m), Bramber (16m). Remaining stations are on the main coast line (see below).

Opening and closure: The line opened as far as Partridge Green 1.7.1861 from a junction with the coast line at Shoreham. The northern section to Itchingfield Junction opened 16.9.1861, the section on to Horsham having opened in 1859. The line closed completely 7.3.1966 except for the section from Shoreham to Beeding Sidings (2¾m), which survived for cement traffic until 1981.

Route and traffic: This was a double-track line of gentle curves running north to south with no severe gradients. Just beyond Partridge Green it met the River Adur, which it crossed three times before reaching the coast line. Trains were push-pull operated except in the final years when modern rolling-stock was introduced and most trains were conventionally operated. Trains ran irregularly, but on average were bi-hourly. Additional trains ran only on the southern end of the line as far as Steyning. Freight traffic was light except on the southern end to Beeding Cement Works, which was far busier.

Horsham to Dorking North (LBSCR)

Station: The only station on the line in West Sussex is Warnham (2m from Horsham).

Opening and closure: Warnham station opened 1.5.1867 with the line.

Route and traffic: This is an undulating line on gentle curves to Warnham and beyond. Traffic is mainly passenger, which continues to this day, with an hourly service. The line was electrified 3.7.1938.

Horsham to Three Bridges (LBSCR)

Stations: Littlehaven Halt (1m from Horsham), Roffey Road Halt (2½m), Faygate (3¼m), Ifield (5¾m), Crawley (7m), Three Bridges (8½m).

Opening and closure: The line and stations opened 14.2.1848, except Ifield (opened as Lyons Crossing Halt but renamed shortly afterwards), Roffey Road Halt, and Littlehaven Halt (opened as Rusper Road Crossing Halt but renamed at the end of 1907), which opened 1.6.1907. Roffey Road Halt closed 3.1.1937. The other stations are still in regular use. Crawley resited 28.7.1968.

Route and traffic: This is a fairly flat and uninteresting line running north-east to Ifield, then east to join the Brighton main line at Three Bridges. There has always been a frequent passenger service, electrified 3.7.1938. There was also considerable freight traffic between Horsham and Three Bridges, and even today there are daily infrastructure trains.

Mid-Sussex line (LBSCR)

Stations: Christ's Hospital (2¼m from Horsham), Itchingfield Junction (no station; 3m), Billingshurst (7¼m), Pulborough (12½m), Hardham Junction (no station; 13½m), Amberley (17¼m), Arundel (20¾m), Ford (23m).

Opening and closure: The line opened from Horsham to Petworth (on the Midhurst branch) 10.10.1859. The line south to Ford, from a new junction at Hardham, opened 3.8.1863. No stations on the Mid-Sussex line have been closed.

Route and traffic: After Itchenfield Junction the line runs south-west as far as Billingshurst, then south to meet the River Arun at Pulborough. This it follows all the way to Ford, through flat but attractive countryside.

Midhurst branches

Pulborough to Midhurst (LBSCR)

Stations: Pulborough (see above, 11m from Midhurst), Fittleworth (8½m), Petworth (5¾m), Selham (3¼m).

Opening and closure: Pulborough to Petworth opened 10.10.1859. Selham opened 1.7.1872. The line from Petworth to Midhurst opened 15.10.1866, but Fittleworth did not open until 2.9.1889. The LBSCR built its own station at Midhurst rather than obtain an agreement to use the LSWR station (see below). It was re-sited 11.7.1881 for ease of operation with the opening of the line to Chichester. The line closed to regular passenger trains 7.2.1955, but was retained for freight and occasional special passenger trains. Freight facilities were withdrawn from Fittleworth and Selham in 5.1963, Midhurst in 10.1963 and Petworth in 5.1966, resulting in complete closure of the line.

Route and traffic: The line passed through the most attractive countryside of the Rother Valley. Fittleworth was only 2ft above sea level and Petworth 5ft. Midhurst is on higher ground and the line approached from the south through a short tunnel. Passenger trains of typical branch line composition ran between Pulborough and Chichester, cut back to Midhurst once the Chichester section was closed (see below). Freight was always light, but sufficient for a service to be retained after withdrawal of passenger services.

Midhurst to Petersfield (LSWR)

Stations: Elsted (3m from Midhurst), Rogate for Harting (5m); Petersfield (9¼m) is in Hampshire.

Opening and closure: The line opened 1.9.1864. A line connecting the LSWR and LBSCR stations at Midhurst opened 17.12.1866, but passengers still had to walk between the two stations. Midhurst (LSWR) closed 12.7.1925 and thereafter all trains used the former LBSCR station. The line closed 7.2.1955.

Route and traffic: The line followed the Rother Valley throughout, with no gradients of any consequence. A push-pull service operated between the two ends of the line and there were no through trains from other parts of the network other than the occasional excursion.

Chichester to Midhurst (LBSCR)

Stations: Chichester (12½m from Midhurst), Lavant (8½m), Singleton (6m), Cocking (2¾m).
Opening and closure: Chichester is on the coast line and opened 8.6.1846. The branch to Midhurst opened 11.7.1881 and closed to passenger traffic 8.7.1935. Freight continued until 11.1951 when flood damage cut off the line just south of Midhurst. This was never repaired but freight continued to run between Chichester and Cocking until 8.1953. The section from Chichester to Lavant was retained for freight until 5.8.1968, re-opened to just short of the station in 2.1972 and closed completely on 15.3.1991.
Route and traffic: The branch left the coast line at Fishbourne Crossing, 1m west of Chichester, and turned north to follow the River Lavant as far as Singleton. The line climbed steadily as it approached the South Downs and passed through a tunnel just south of Singleton, and two more between Singleton and Cocking. As with the other lines to Midhurst, there were no regular through trains from other parts of the railway system and typical branch line stock and motive power was used. Freight traffic was light and once the line had been completely closed north of Lavant, was mainly of a seasonal nature. This changed with the opening of a stone quarry at Lavant, when daily trains were run between Lavant and Drayton (see section on 'South Coast line' below).

Brighton main line: Three Bridges to Hassocks (LBSCR)

Stations: Three Bridges (29¼m from Victoria), Balcombe (33¾m), Copyhold Junction (no station; 36¼m), Haywards Heath (37¾m), Wivelsfield (40½m), Burgess Hill (41½m), Hassocks (43½m). The remaining stations are in East Sussex.

Opening and closure: The line opened as part of the main line to Brighton as far as Haywards Heath 12.7.1841. South from Haywards Heath opened 21.9.1841. Wivelsfield opened as Keymer Junction 1.8.1886 and was renamed 1.7.1896. Hassocks was known as Hassocks Gate until 1.10.1881. None of the stations have closed.
Route and traffic: The line was built to main-line standards with no sharp curves or steep gradients, enabling fast running over long stretches. There are tunnels between Three Bridges and Balcombe and at Clayton just before the county boundary. The Ouse Valley Viaduct is just north of Copyhold Junction. This has always been primarily a passenger line with fast and frequent trains between London and Brighton. It was electrified from Three Bridges 1.1.1933. There has never been heavy freight traffic, and the only trains now regularly seen convey stone from Ardingly northward after reversal at Haywards Heath.

Lines from East Grinstead (LBSCR)

Three Bridges to East Grinstead

Stations: Rowfant (2¼m from Three Bridges), Grange Road (4m), East Grinstead (6¾m).
Opening and closure: The line opened 9.7.1855, but Grange Road was not opened until 2.4.1860. East Grinstead station was re-sited from 1.10.1866 and again from 1.8.1882. The line closed completely 2.1.1967.
Route and traffic: This pleasant line passed through wooded countryside most of the way, once clear of the outskirts of Three Bridges and East Grinstead. It turned sharply east on leaving Three Bridges and climbed at 1 in 88 for about 1½ miles. It continued to run east over Crawley Down encountering a total of three level crossings. Passenger services ran between Three Bridges and Tunbridge Wells West with a few trains with portions to and from London. Many of the trains were push-pull operated and exclusively so in later years when the service ran only as far as East Grinstead. Even in BR days there were occasional special through trains. Rowfant

had a siding to a brickworks, which generated some traffic. A fuel storage depot was later built at Rowfant and this also used rail transport. This continued to be served after closure of the line, as an extended siding from Three Bridges.

East Grinstead to Lewes

Stations: East Grinstead (30m from Victoria), Kingscote (32m), West Hoathly (34m), Horsted Keynes (36¼m), Horsted Keynes Bluebell Halt (36½m), Holywell Halt (37¼m), Freshfield Halt (38¾m). The remaining stations are in East Sussex.

Ardingly (38½m) was on the branch from Horsted Keynes to Haywards Heath.

Opening and closure: The line opened from East Grinstead (new station) to the junction with the Uckfield-Lewes line at Culver Junction 1.8.1882, and closed officially 13.6.1955, although the last service train ran 28.5.1955. Occasional special passenger trains ran on part of the line until 1959. Horsted Keynes remained open for the passenger service from Seaford via Haywards Heath and Copyhold Junction. East Grinstead-Lewes services were re-instated 7.8.1956, except at Kingscote (and Barcombe), which remained closed. A second closure of the line took place 16.3.1958, again excluding Horsted Keynes. Sheffield Park saw its first passenger train under the auspices of the Bluebell Railway 7.8.1960 and trains ran to the newly constructed Horsted Keynes Bluebell Halt. Holywell Halt (opened 1.4.1962, closed 1963) and Freshfield Halt were also built by the Bluebell Railway. All these halts are now closed. The first Bluebell Railway passenger train ran into Horsted Keynes (LBSCR station) 29.10.1961. Kingscote re-opened 23.4.1994.

The Ardingly line opened 3.9.1883 and was electrified 7.7.1935. Passenger services were withdrawn 28.10.1963, and the section between Horsted Keynes and Ardingly has been dismantled.

Route and traffic: The line leaves East Grinstead on Imberhorne Viaduct and descends to Kingscote, then after a short level stretch climbs to West Hoathly and thereafter descends almost all the way to Freshfield Halt

and beyond. Much of this is at 1 in 75, including West Hoathly Tunnel. Some of the passenger trains ran from London, others started either at Oxted or East Grinstead. The service re-instated by BR ran only from East Grinstead and did not include Kingscote. The present-day service runs between Kingscote and Sheffield Park. There was a regular pick-up goods train and this is occasionally recreated for historical interest. Some of the through trains from London took the Ardingly branch to Brighton. These trains were steam operated and were in addition to the regular electric train service that ran between Horsted Keynes and Seaford. Stone trains still use the line on a regular basis between Ardingly and Haywards Heath. There is no longer a junction at Copyhold.

South Coast line (LBSCR)

Stations: Southbourne Halt (11¼m from Portsmouth Harbour), Nutbourne Halt (12¼m), Bosham (13¾m), Fishbourne Halt (15¼m), Chichester (16¾m), Drayton (18¾m), Woodgate for Bognor (21¾m), Barnham Junction (23m), Yapton (24½m), Ford (25¾m), Arundel & Littlehampton (27½m), Angmering (30m), Goring-by-Sea (32½m), West Worthing (34¼m), Worthing Central (35m), Ham Bridge Halt (35¾m), Lancing (37¼m), Bungalow Town Halt (38½m), Shoreham-by-Sea (39½m), Southwick (41m), Fishersgate Halt (42m). The remaining stations are in East Sussex.

There are branches to Bognor Regis (3½m from Barnham) and Littlehampton (2m from Ford).

Opening and closure: The line opened between Havant (8m from Portsmouth Harbour and in Hampshire) and Chichester 15.3.1847. Chichester to Ford (called Arundel until 5.1850) opened 8.6.1846. Littlehampton & Arundel to Worthing opened 16.3.1846. At the same time Littlehampton & Arundel was renamed Littlehampton, to be changed again in 5.1850 to Arundel & Littlehampton. The branch to Littlehampton opened 17.8.1863. An improved layout between Angmering and

Ford opened 1.1.1887. Worthing to Shoreham opened 24.11.1845, and Shoreham to Brighton 12.5.1840. Several stations were added after the various sections of the line were opened: West Worthing opened 4.11.1889, Fishersgate and Ham Bridge Halts 3.9.1905, Southbourne, Nutbourne and Fishbourne Halts 1.4.1906, and Bungalow Town Halt 1.7.1935.

The branch to Bognor opened 1.6.1864 with the opening of Barnham. At the same time Woodgate for Bognor closed.

Arundel & Littlehampton closed 1.9.1863, but a halt called Lyminster was opened on the site 1.8.1907, closing in 9.1914. Yapton closed 1.6.1864. Drayton closed 1.6.1930. Ham Bridge Halt was renamed East Worthing Halt 23.5.1949. Bungalow Town Halt was later renamed Shoreham Airport and closed 15.7.1940.

Bognor to Worthing was electrified 22.5.1938 and Worthing to Brighton 1.1.1933. The Littlehampton branch and the coast line west to Havant were electrified 3.7.1938.

Route and traffic: The line follows closely the coast itself and passes through an area of dense population, which significantly increases with visitors during the summer months. The passenger services are well patronised by local residents, visitors and longer-distance travellers, for example from Southampton and Portsmouth to Brighton and further east. There is also heavy traffic to and from London. There is a proliferation of level crossings, currently more than 30 on the coast line within West Sussex.

The Dyke branch (LBSCR)

Stations: Rowan Halt (2½m from Brighton), Golf Club Halt (4¾m), both in East Sussex; The Dyke (5½m).

Opening and closure: The line opened 1.9.1887. Rowan Halt opened 18.12.1933. Golf Club Halt was private. The line closed 1.1.1917, re-opened 26.7.1920, and closed finally 1.1.1939.

Route and traffic: The line climbed at 1 in 40 almost all the way to The Dyke from the junction with the coast line (just west of present-day Aldrington Halt). It was built mainly as a tourist line but goods was also carried. There was a frequent service usually provided by a single coach, the engine running round at The Dyke. For a short period a steam railbus was used.

London Brighton and South
Coast Railway

——————

Partridge Green to

Rowfant

INDEX OF LOCATIONS

Page numbers in **bold** refer to the photographs; other entries refer to the Gazetteer section.